First Look at Languages

My First Look at German

by Jenna Lee Gleisner

bucket
der Eimer
(DE-uh EYE-muh)

shovel
die Schaufel
(DEE SHA-o-ful)

Bullfrog Books

Ideas for Parents and Teachers

Bullfrog Books let children practice reading informational text at the earliest reading levels. Repetition, familiar words, and photo labels support early readers.

Before Reading

- Discuss the cover photo. What does it tell them?
- Read through the introduction on page 4 and book guide on page 5.

Read the Book

- "Walk" through the book and look at the photos. Let the child ask questions. Point out the photo labels. Sound out the words together.
- Read the book to the child, or have him or her read independently.

After Reading

- Prompt the child to think more. Ask: Have you heard or spoken German before? Practice saying the German words in this book.

Bullfrog Books are published by Jump!
5357 Penn Avenue South
Minneapolis, MN 55419
www.jumplibrary.com

Library of Congress Cataloging-in-Publication Data

Names: Gleisner, Jenna Lee, author.
Title: My first look at German / by Jenna Lee Gleisner.
Description: Minneapolis, MN: Jump!, Inc., [2020]
Series: First look at languages | Includes index.
Audience: Ages: 5–8 | Audience: Grades: K–1
Identifiers: LCCN 2019031222 (print)
LCCN 2019031223 (ebook)
ISBN 9781645273059 (hardcover)
ISBN 9781645273066 (ebook)
Subjects: LCSH: German language—Textbooks for foreign speakers—English—Juvenile literature.
Classification: LCC PF3112 .G575 2020 (print) |
LCC PF3112 (ebook) | DDC 438.2/421—dc23
LC record available at https://lccn.loc.gov/2019031222
LC ebook record available at https://lccn.loc.gov/2019031223

Editor: Jenna Trnka
Designer: Michelle Sonnek
Translator: Anne-Sophie Seidler

Photo Credits: Alfa Photostudio/Shutterstock, cover (top left); Jakob Dam Knudsen/Shutterstock, cover (bottom left); Gemenacom/Shutterstock, cover (right); DenisNata/Shutterstock, 1; Nataliia K/Shutterstock, 3; LAURA_VN/Shutterstock, 5; Pixel-Shot/Shutterstock, 6, 14; oatzpenz studio/Shutterstock, 7; sergeykot/Shutterstock, 8–9; Eric Isselee/Shutterstock, 10; 11 (dog); Dora Zett/Shutterstock, 11 (cat); Susan Schmitz/Shutterstock, 11 (snake); Africa Studio/Shutterstock, 12–13; wavebreakmedia/Shutterstock, 14–15; matt _ dela/iStock, 16–17; New Africa/Shutterstock, 18–19; UV70/Shutterstock, 20–21 (place setting); Joe Gough/Shutterstock, 20–21 (meal); Yeti studio/Shutterstock, 24.

Printed in the United States of America at Corporate Graphics in North Mankato, Minnesota.

Table of Contents

Introduction to German 4

Book Guide 5

Let's Learn German! 6

Phrases to Know 22

Colors 23

Numbers 23

Index 24

To Learn More 24

boots
die Stiefel
(DEE SHTEE-ful)

Introduction to German

Where Is German Spoken?

German is spoken in Germany, Austria, Switzerland, Belgium, Liechtenstein, and Luxembourg.

How It Differs from English

- The German language uses the same alphabet as English.

- But it has one letter that doesn't exist in English. The "ß" is called "sharp S." It is a double "s" sound.

- In German, all nouns begin with a capital letter, even if they are in the middle of a sentence! It looks like this: "Die Katze ist im Haus." (The cat is in the house.)

Umlaut

Some vowels appear with two dots: ä, ö, ü. This is called the umlaut. It changes the pronunciation of the letter or the meaning of the word. For example, "Vogel" means "bird," but "Vögel" with an umlaut means "birds."

You can speak German, too! Let's learn!

Book Guide

This book follows Ben during a typical day. He speaks German. We will learn what his family members, teachers, and friends are called in German. We will also learn the German words for common items we see and use every day.

There are three labels for each word. The first is the English word. The second is the German word. The third is how we pronounce, or say, it. The stressed syllable is in uppercase.

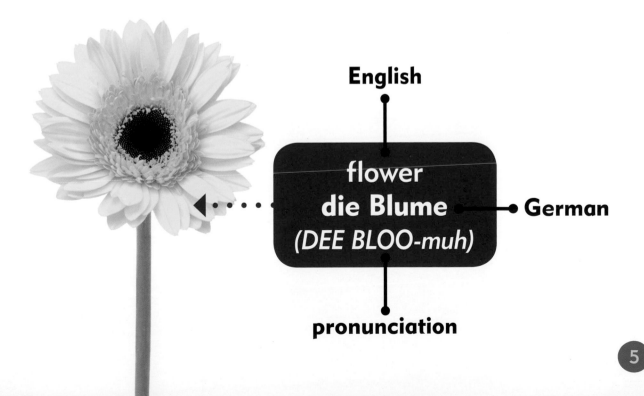

English

flower
die Blume
(DEE BLOO-muh)

German

pronunciation

Let's Learn German!

This is Ben.

He speaks German.

Let's learn!

German

Deutsch

(DOY-tsh)

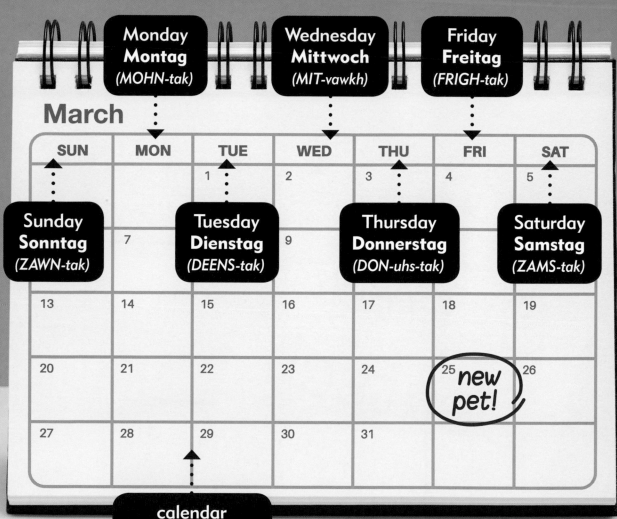

Monday
Montag
(MOHN-tak)

Wednesday
Mittwoch
(MIT-vawkh)

Friday
Freitag
(FRIGH-tak)

March

SUN	MON	TUE	WED	THU	FRI	SAT
		1	2	3	4	5
	7		9			
13	14	15	16	17	18	19
20	21	22	23	24	25 new pet!	26
27	28	29	30	31		

Sunday
Sonntag
(ZAWN-tak)

Tuesday
Dienstag
(DEENS-tak)

Thursday
Donnerstag
(DON-uhs-tak)

Saturday
Samstag
(ZAMS-tak)

calendar
der Kalender
(DE-uh ka-LEN-deuh)

8

Today is an exciting day!

Why?

Ben's family is getting a new pet!

What pet would you choose?

Can you say it in German?

Practice!

bird
der Vogel
(DE-uh FOH-gul)

fish
der Fisch
(DE-uh FISH)

pets
die Haustiere
(DEE HOWSS-TEER-uh)

cat
die Katze
(DEE KAT-suh)

dog
der Hund
(DE-uh HOONT)

snake
die Schlange
(DEE SHLANG-uh)

11

family
die Familie
(DEE fa-MEE-lyuh)

father
der Vater
(DE-uh FA-tuh)

sister
die Schwester
(DEE SHVES-tuh)

brother
der Bruder
(DE-uh BROO-duh)

mother
die Mutter
(DEE MOOT-uh)

12

Ben's family chooses
a cat!

They name it Ginger.

Ben draws a picture of Ginger.

He brings it to school.

He shows his friends.

picture
das Bild
(DAS BILT)

pencil
der Bleistift
(DE-uh BLEYE-shtif-t)

classroom
das Klassenzimmer
(DAS KLASS-un-TSIM-muh)

friend
die Freundin
(DEE FROYN-din)

teacher
der Lehrer
(DE-uh LEH-ruh)

book
das Buch
(DAS BOOKH)

paper
das Papier
(DAS pa-PEE-uh)

15

tree
der Baum
(DE-uh BA-om)

sky
der Himmel
(DE-uh HIMM-ul)

bus
der Bus
(DE-uh BOOS)

SCHOOL BUS

road
die Straße
(DEE SH-TRAH-suh)

grass
das Gras
(DAS GRAHSS)

16

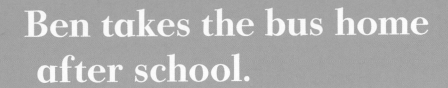

Ben takes the bus home after school.

Bus is spelled the same in German.

But it sounds different. Practice saying it!

school
die Schule
(DEE SHOO-luh)

This is Ben's bedroom.

He likes the color blue.

Can you say it
in German?

blue
blau
(BLA-O)

18

pillow
das Kopfkissen
(DAS KOPF-kiss-uhn)

bedroom
das Schlafzimmer
(DAS SHLAHF-tsim-muh)

bed
das Bett
(DAS BET)

desk
der Schreibtisch
(DE-uh sh-REYE-b-tish)

chair
der Stuhl
(DE-uh sh-TOOL)

rug
der Teppich
(DE-uh TE-pee-sh)

19

dinner
das Abendessen
(DAS A-buhnt-ESS-uhn)

peas
die Erbsen
(DEE ERB-suhn)

plate
der Teller
(DE-uh TELL-uh)

potatoes
die Kartoffeln
(DEE kar-TOFF-uln)

fork
die Gabel
(DEE GAH-bul)

meatball
die Frikadelle
(DEE free-ka-DEL-uh)

Ben eats dinner.

Then he will play with Ginger!

Fun!

knife
das Messer
(DAS MESS-uh)

Phrases to Know

Hello!
Hallo!
(HAL-oh)

Goodbye!
Auf Wiedersehen!
(OWF VEE-duh-zay-hen)

Yes.
Ja.
(YA)

No.
Nein.
(NINE)

Thank you!
Danke!
(DAN-kuh)

You're welcome!
Bitte!
(BIT-uh)

My name is _____.
Mein Name ist _____.
(MINE NAH-muh IST)

How are you?
Wie geht es dir?
(Vee GEHT es dee-uh)

Colors

red **rot** *(ROHT)*	orange **orange** *(o-RANCH)*	yellow **gelb** *(GELP)*	green **grün** *(GRUUN)*	blue **blau** *(BLA-O)*
purple **lila** *(LEE-la)*	pink **rosa** *(ROH-za)*	brown **braun** *(BROWN)*	gray **grau** *(GRA-O)*	black **schwarz** *(sh-VAR-tss)*

Numbers

1 **eins** *(EYE-nss)*	**2** **zwei** *(tss-VEYE)*	**3** **drei** *(DRY)*	**4** **vier** *(FEER)*	**5** **fünf** *(FUUN-f)*
6 **sechs** *(ZEKSS)*	**7** **sieben** *(ZEE-bun)*	**8** **acht** *(AKHT)*	**9** **neun** *(NOY-n)*	**10** **zehn** *(TSS-ehn)*

Index

bedroom 18

bus 17

cat 13

day 9

dinner 21

family 9, 13

friends 14

pet 9, 10

picture 14

school 14, 17

cheese
der Käse
(DE-uh KEH-zuh)

To Learn More

Finding more information is as easy as 1, 2, 3.

❶ Go to www.factsurfer.com

❷ Enter "myfirstlookatGerman" into the search box.

❸ Click the "Surf" button to see a list of websites.